GOD the Thought of It First!

by Joan N. Keener

illustrated by Stephen Carpenter

The Standard Publishing Company, Cincinnati, Ohio. A division of Standex International Corporation.
© 1996 by The Standard Publishing Company. Printed in the United States of America. All rights reserved.
Designed by Coleen Davis. Typography by Dale E. Meyers and Diane Stortz.
Library of Congress Catalog Card Number 95-37055. Cataloging-in-Publication data available.
ISBN 0-7847-0453-8.

Scripture on page 24 from the *International Children's Bible*, New Century Version.
© 1986, 1989 by Word Publishing, Dallas, Texas 75039. Used by permission.

STANDARD
PUBLISHING
Cincinnati, Ohio

Our world is full of fun and helpful things made from materials like wood, metal, plastic, and cloth.
Each one began with an *idea*.

God has the *best* ideas. In the beginning, God made the heavens and the earth — out of *nothing!* Yes, our world is full of things that began as good ideas . . .

but GOD is the one who thought of them first!

A **helicopter** on a rescue mission flies up or down, backward or forward, and hovers in the air.

But GOD the Creator thought of it first!

He made the . . .

HUMMINGBIRD

His wings beat *fast* and cause a humming sound.
Hummingbirds can fly up or down, backward or forward,
and they can hover in the air.

A **submarine** has special tanks that fill with water to make the sub sink. When the water is pumped out of the tanks, the sub rises.

But GOD the Creator thought of it first!

He made the . . .

CHAMBERED NAUTILUS

The bones of this sea creature form small "rooms," or chambers. The chambers empty or fill with water to make the little nautilus go up or down.

To walk over soft, deep snow
without sinking, you wear **snowshoes**.
And **snowboots** keep your feet warm.

But GOD the Creator thought of it first!

He made the . . .

SNOWSHOE RABBIT

His wide feet keep him on top of the snow. Long hairs grow on the sides of his feet and between his toes. The hairs help the rabbit's feet stay warm.

When you swim underwater, you can breathe with a **snorkel**.

But GOD the Creator thought of it first!

He made the . . .

ELEPHANT

He breathes through his trunk
when he goes swimming!

When you ride your bike or roller-skate, you wear a **helmet** and **knee pads** for protection.

But GOD the Creator thought of it first!

He made the . . .

ARMADILLO

Hard plates protect this creature's body. The plates are jointed, so he can roll up in a ball for extra safety.

If you want to hang a sun catcher in a window, you use a **suction cup.**

But GOD the Creator thought of it first!

He made the . . .

OCTOPUS

Two rows of suction cups on each arm
help the octopus to stick tight to anything.

When you travel in a **camper**, you are taking your home with you.

But GOD the Creator thought of it first!

He made the . . .

TURTLE

His moveable home is his shell. He takes it with him
wherever he goes, and sometimes he stays inside all day!

A **baby carrier** lets parents keep their babies with them wherever they go.

But GOD the Creator thought of it first!

He made the . . .

KANGAROO

A mother kangaroo keeps her baby, called a "joey," in a pouch on the front of her body. She takes the little joey with her wherever she goes.

Suspended under long "wings" made of cloth, the pilot of a **hang glider** flies from place to place.

But GOD the Creator thought of it first!

He made the . . .

FLYING SQUIRREL

To glide from tree to tree,
he spreads out the folds of skin
between his front and back legs.

A jumbo jet airplane is pushed through the sky by its huge **jet-propelled engines.**

**But GOD the Creator
thought of it first!**

He made the . . .

GIANT SQUID

To move through the ocean, he takes water into a special part of his body and then forcefully jets it out.

Ask the animals, and they will teach you.
Or ask the birds of the air,
and they will tell you.
Speak to the earth, and it will teach you.
Or let the fish of the sea tell you.
Every one of these knows that the hand
of the Lord has done this.
Job 12:7-9

Remember,
our world is full of things that
began as good ideas, but . . .

GOD is the one who thought of them first!

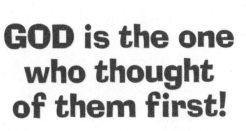

For many years, Joan Keener has collected
examples like the ones in this book. She would
like to hear from readers who have examples
to share with her. Write to Joan Keener in care
of Standard Publishing, Children's Books,
8121 Hamilton Avenue, Cincinnati, OH 45231.